WriteType:
Personality Types and Writing Styles

STEPHEN D. GLADIS

Published By
Human Resource Development Press, Inc.
    22 Amherst Road
    Amherst, Massachusetts 01002
    (413) 253-3488 (Mass.)
    1-800-822-2801 (outside Mass.)

ISBN 0-87425-221-0

First printing May 1993

DEDICATION

To the memory of my parents, Steve and Margaret Gladis, who always strove to guide and educate me. While neither of them knew about personality types or WriteType, I think Dad was an ISTJ and Mom was an ENFJ. Thanks to Dad for the gifts of discipline and perseverance and to Mom for giving me a creative streak and the love of people. Now I understand—thanks.

ABOUT THE AUTHOR

Dr. Stephen D. Gladis is an FBI Special Agent. He received his Doctorate in Education from George Mason University and has served as both the chief of speechwriting and publications for the FBI. Dr. Gladis teaches writing and communications courses and is an adjunct professor at George Mason University, the University of Virginia, and Trinity College. He has published numerous journal and magazine articles as well as five other books: *Survival Writing, Survival Communication, ProcessWriting, The Ten Commandments for Public Speakers,* and *ProcessWriting Workshop.*

ACKNOWLEDGMENTS

To those who reviewed, edited, and advised me: Aleks Nelson, Pat Solley, Ray McElhaney, Bobbi Cotter, Robin Dinerman, Robbin Zeff, Margo Moser, Julie Linkins, and Beth Farish.

To Dianna Gibb, George Jensen, and Sue Scanlon who helped me more accurately adapt personality type to writing by their careful reviews of this book.

To my wife, Donna, and my children, Kimberly and Jessica, who tolerated me during this obsession.

Many thanks to you all.

TABLE OF CONTENTS

CHAPTER I

AN INTRODUCTION TO PERSONALITY TYPE

I wrote this book to help people who have to write on the job. It's not intended for professional writers, journalists, scholars, or linguists. It's for engineers, doctors, lawyers, accountants, computer programmers, nurses, social workers and so many others who need to write to get things done. It's also for managers who direct people to write and who need to know how best to use those different writers.

In this book I will demonstrate how people with different personality types approach writing very differently and how diversity in writing is not just healthy, but also necessary.

You might be legitimately asking, "Yes, but how is this helpful to me—how can I use such knowledge?" The answer is that, armed with such information, your writing can be clearer, more effective, and more persuasive. You can improve not only your own writing immeasurably, but also the writing of others in your organization.

Before you came to your organization, you were taught to write somewhere—usually at school under the tutelage of a composition teacher. It was then that many of us, while learning to write, also learned to fear and even to hate writing. Often, well meaning teachers taught us how to write "the correct way"—their way. They may even have caused us to doubt our own abilities, especially if we did not think or write "the correct way" naturally. Let me demonstrate what I'm talking about by telling you a short story about how I learned to write.

Sister Mary Immaculate Conception

I went to a Catholic grammar school and learned to write from a woman named Sister Mary Immaculate Conception. A nice enough woman, I'm now sure; but at the time, she was feared by even the bravest of young turks in our class. She was a woman of God—stern, resolute, dedicated. She had a steely logic about her that might have intimidated Aristotle or Aquinas. A woman of definite conviction, she predictably had a strong theory about how people, students in particular, should write. And, she imposed this theory on all who fell under her tutelage.

I fell under her care and was subjected to her writing theory, which went something like this: writing, like all things, belongs to God, and God deserves the best— perfection. Indeed, perfection was her watchword. She wanted perfect grammar, spelling, punctuation, logic— you name it, and she wanted it now. Unfortunately, I knew of few perfect students—least of all, me.

So, I had more than my share of problems with Sister Mary. First, I could not, and still cannot, spell worth a nickel. I became an author despite this spelling problem. Indeed, I think being able to spell a word only one way shows a certain lack of imagination—at least that's how I rationalize it. My saving grace came when spell-checking programs hit the market. What a relief—"Sister-on-a-Floppy" programs.

Second, I was not the most logical boy: passion possessed me, and logic eluded me. Sister Mary was a steely-eyed bastion of both restraint and logic. She required outlines and logical plans of writing for every composition we wrote. This gave me major problems. I never, even to this day, have been totally comfortable with outlines. So, I often wrote papers first and then wrote the outlines to fit the papers. All the while, I felt abnormal because, to listen to Sister Mary, you'd think that everybody thought her way. Not me.

Third, whenever she gave us a writing assignment, I usually turned to the kids near me to strike up a conversation about my topic. I liked to talk about my writing and still do—even if it means talking out loud to myself. There has always been an external nature to my writing that makes it come alive for me and for my audience. Keeping ideas inside was nearly intolerable. Needless to say, Sister Mary—a contemplative type—did not appreciate anyone talking in class. Have you ever been struck on the knuckles with a ruler? She taught that students must think to themselves long and hard before they write, and she strictly forbade talking because, to her, getting any "help" from others was not only illegal, but even worse, a sin.

I suspect that my experience with Sister Mary Immaculate Conception is painfully similar to that of many youngsters who were forced to learn from the perspective of their individual teachers. Parents, teachers, bosses, and authority figures all seem to have a preferred approach to everything—including writing. Unfortunately, few realize that our brains are all wired differently. Each one of us approaches life's tasks uniquely and, therefore, teaching writing by using one particular approach will severely limit the potential to teach to most of the known world. Sister Mary frustrated the hell (literally) out of many of the kids. Those kids who thought exactly like the good Sister had no problems and sailed through the class. Others, like me, had a bumpier trip. I'm sure we made Sister Mary's ride a little uncomfortable as well.

This book is an attempt to smooth the journey for those to whom writing is part of the daily work world. It tries to match different learning methods with different personality types to facilitate the writing process.

Writing personality type, or WriteType, is what this book is all about. Thanks to the work of Carl Jung, as well as Katherine Briggs and Isabel Myers, we have learned much about how different people approach life and about how we all bring different gifts to the table. Indeed, the collective works of Jung, Myers and Briggs, and others recognize, use and celebrate those differences, rather than try to homogenize them in order to make all people think and act alike. This book will not try to develop any homogenized writing style—quite the opposite. I suggest that, because we all have distinctive personality types, we all also have different writing styles. Recognizing that, I will suggest that we try to use our strengths, develop our weaknesses, and always recognize that different is not bad, but both good and useful to the writing process.

To help give some insight into what you'll be learning as you read this book, here is an overview of its contents.

Overview

Chapter II, **Understanding Personality Type**, describes eight dimensions of personality and how they affect, even determine, what people do. The Thumbnail Personality Sketch will determine your own personality type.

Chapter III, **The Four Basic Writing Types**, explains the four types of writers: correspondents, technical writers, creative writers, and analytical writers. This chapter also describes the strengths and weaknesses of each type.

Chapter IV, **Personality Type and the Writing Process**, describes how each writing type approaches the writing process in each of its major steps: prewriting, drafting, and editing.

Chapter V, **Personality Within the Organization**, teaches you where and how to spot various personality types in an organization, what kinds of jobs people with these personality types are likely to gravitate to, and what kinds of things they say that reveal their types.

Chapter VI, **Collaborative Writing Groups**, explains the power of groups in writing, how to form groups, how to conduct a writing group session, and how the Four

Basic Writing Types respond to others' writings, as well as how they react to criticism of their own writing.

Chapter VII, **The Care and Feeding of Personality Types**, provides you with coaching tips and preferred assignments of the various writing types.

Chapter VIII, **Q & A About WriteType**, answers most commonly asked questions about WriteType and personality types. It also provides you with additional resources if you wish to pursue the topic further.

CHAPTER II

UNDERSTANDING PERSONALITY TYPE

"He's the strong silent type." "Still waters run deep." "She's an open book." "He wears his heart on his sleeve." These and many more sayings permeate our culture. Each, in its own way, attempts to do what we all inherently try to do: describe someone's personality type. While the process of trying to fit a person's personality type into one box seems fatally flawed from the outset, because there are so many social, psychological, and cultural variables, the urge remains to figure each other out.

Why? I suppose it's because we seek a consistent method to deal with people and life's decisions. We all recognize that, in spite of real differences, certain recurring traits, characteristics, or functions consistently surface. For example, Swiss psychiatrist Carl Jung recognized that people were different, not because of some underlying psychological deficiency, but because of personality differences or preferences. He developed a theory of personality types in his book, *Personality Types* (1921). Jung theorized that there were two components of type—attitudes (extravert vs. introvert) and functions (sensation vs. intuition and thinking vs. feeling). Isabel Myers and Katherine Briggs later contributed two additional attitudes (judgment vs. perception) to the theory of personality.

These four pairs of personality dimensions comprise the core of understanding personality development and will be covered in this chapter.

Personality Dimensions

Basic Source of Energy: Extraversion (E) vs. Introversion (I)

Jung goes to great lengths in his book to explain how extraverts and introverts relate to life and gain energy in dramatically different ways.

Extraverts engage their external world as a means of coming to understanding. They reach out and embrace the external, both people and objects. When given a problem, they reach out to people and objects for information and answers. They tend to be sociable and gain energy by being with other people. They are doers— taking action, sometimes too impulsively, when confronted with a problem. At ease with people, they generally have a facility for communication and interaction, especially in a group setting. Extraverts dislike being alone and will seek out a group, especially to learn new information, solve a problem, or complete a task. Because of their external orientation, extraverts talk to hear what they are thinking. They think as they talk.

Extravert Indicator

An extravert might say:

"I'm only thinking out loud."
"I'm bored, let's go shopping or find a good party."
"Love me, hate me, but don't ignore me."

On the other hand, introverts get energy by drawing within themselves. They energize more by being alone than by being with other people. They tend to think about problems before reaching out to others. At ease with being alone, introverts are self-reliant and contemplative. They first respond inwardly, not outwardly like extraverts. They choose their words carefully. They think, then talk.

Introvert Indicator

An introvert might say:

"At last, time for some peace and quiet."
"I need time to think over what you just said."
"I'm content just to be left alone."

Ways of Knowing: Sensing (S) and iNtuition (N)

According to Jung, people come to know and to learn through one of two functions: sensing or intuition. Let's call them, therefore, sensors (S) and iNtuitors (N) [emphasized this way to distinguish it from introverts (I)]. Sensors come to know through their senses. To them life is a factual reality. If they can see, touch, taste, smell, and/or hear something, they believe it exists. They are extremely here-and-now oriented, not much interested in the future, but rather in the past and/or present. Why? Because they can objectively and scientifically determine that something exists or existed through their senses. They like routines, tried-and-true solutions or approaches to problems; they eschew the novel, the imaginative, the innovative in favor of the traditional, the observable, the standard.

Sensor Indicator

A sensor might say:

"Show me, and I'll believe you."
"Give me facts, not fantasy."
"If it ain't broke, don't fix it."

On the other hand, iNtuitors come to knowledge very differently than sensors. An iNtuitor learns more indirectly by filtering perceptions through an unconscious, integrative, global process, which produces new and creative insights and ideas from sensory input. Indeed, iNtuitors are able to learn from what goes on beyond the senses. As such, iNtuitors live not for today but for tomorrow. They ask not about what is or what was, but what will be or what could be. They are imaginative, creative, and like solving new problems. They dislike the traditional or the standard and are given to the novel, imaginative, and innovative aspects of life.

iNtuitor Indicator

An iNtuitor might say:

"I just have a gut feeling that something's wrong."
"Let's try something completely new."
"I have an idea!"

Ways of Deciding: Thinking (T) vs. Feeling (F)

Once information is gathered, either through the senses or through an intuitive process, that information is acted on or decided upon through the use of two other functions: thinking or feeling.

Thinkers prefer logic and analysis over feelings and values. They filter sensory and intuitive information through logic to make sense out of the data. They draw conclusions based on a logical and analytical, but impersonal, process. They remain objective, analytically question others' conclusions, and are more truthful than tactful.

Thinking Indicator

A thinker might say:

"Is this fair?"
"It's wrong, fix it."
"What's your rationale for believing that?"

Feelers decide differently than thinkers. Feelers prefer subjective values to objective analysis and are personal rather than impersonal when dealing with people. They are rooted in the values of society and people, and as such they rely on a more subjective reasoning process than do thinkers.

Unlike thinkers, feelers make decisions based on emotion and values, and they give less weight to objective logic and analysis, especially where logic might offend established values or feelings. Feelers are people oriented, understand audiences well, are warm hearted, contribute to group rapport, and have a high penchant for acceptance and affiliation. They tend to be more tactful than truthful, especially when delivering bad news.

Feeler Indicator

A feeler might say:

"I hope we don't offend him."
"Let's approach this from the customer's
    point of view."
"People are our most important product."

Orientation to the Outer World: Judgment (J) vs. Perception (P)

Along with Jung, two exceptional women, Katherine Briggs and her daughter Isabel Briggs Myers, worked tirelessly to explain seemingly random personality types in society. Ultimately, Isabel Myers developed the Myers-Briggs Type Indicator (MBTI), and after years of research her MBTI was published in 1962 by Educational Testing Service.

While Myers and Briggs followed Jung's teachings closely, they added another aspect to his model of personality: orientation to the outer world. This orientation to the outer world breaks down into two attitudes: judgment (J) and perception (P). These additions mark a significant contribution to Jung's theory of personality development.

In terms of orientation to the outer world, judgers are more concerned with closure than curiosity. Judgers like to plan; they like certainty; they avoid ambiguity. They prefer to settle matters, complete projects, and move on to new ones. They make lists, scratch out accomplishments, and are, in short, the "doers" of life. Judgers take in only as much information as they need to make a decision and then proceed, at times without enough information, to make the best decision. With a strong commitment to closure, judgers are almost fanatical about completing things on or before the deadline. Judgers project a sense of organization and decisiveness.

Judger Indicator

> A Judger might say:
>
> "Just do it."
> "No surprises please."
> "That's not on my schedule."

Perceivers, on the other hand, favor curiosity to closure. They may be thought of as "infomaniacs"— desiring more and more information before ever being ready to make a decision. Unlike the planned life of the judgers, perceivers live a life of spontaneity. As such, they can handle the unexpected and adapt with ease and grace. Continually open to incoming data, perceivers are flexible, receptive, and tolerant. They are extemporaneous and seem to enjoy the day-to-day living so often neglected by the more planned and future-oriented judger.

Perceiver Indicator

> A Perceiver might say:
>
> "Take life one day at a time."
> "I just need a little more information to
>   decide."
> "Last minute changes—no problem."

Personality and Writing

Personality and writing are closely linked. In fact, I believe you can't accurately talk about how people write unless you understand their personalties. Therefore, determining your personality type will help you understand your writing, as well as the writing of others.

Personality indicators have been developed over the years to help people determine their types. The most established and widely recognized as most reliable, is the MBTI. Available only through a certified MBTI administrator, the Indicator comes in several forms—Form F, Form G, and the abbreviated Form G (which can be self-scored). The MBTI is considered to be the most reliable of all the indicators because it has been the most researched and validated. The foundation for MBTI theory rests with the gathering of information and decision making—cognitive thinking styles. These cognitive styles represent the choices of preference between Sensing vs. iNtuition and Thinking vs. Feeling; therefore, the core of the MBTI approach to personality typing is comprised of the function groups: SF, ST, NF, NT. This approach will also explain the Four Basic Writing Types (see Chapter III) later in this book.

Thumbnail Personality Sketch

To accurately determine your personality type, you may want to take the MBTI from a certified administrator. However, for the time being, you may want a clue about your own personality type, so that what you read about writing in this book will be more personally relevant. To help you, I have developed the Thumbnail Personality Sketch (TPS). I have drawn together a table of descriptors for each of the eight personality dimensions: Extraversion (E) vs. Introversion (I); Sensing (S) vs. iNtuition (N); Thinking (T) vs. Feeling (F); and Perception (P) vs. Judging (J). To take the TPS, read each of the four pairs and decide which dimension of each is your preferred one while you are at work. After you've decided your preference for each dimension, assign number values to the dimensions of each pair that add up to a total of 7. For example, if you recognize that you are extremely outgoing, give yourself a 6 or 7 in E and a 1 or 0 for I. If you are a moderately deadline-driven list maker, give yourself a 5 or 4 in J, and a 2 or 3 in P. These decisions must be a forced choice, meaning that even if you believe you're equally split between two dimensions, you must decide. For example, if you believe that you are equally extraverted (E) and introverted (I) in work situations, you must decide, based on the descriptions, which one of those two (Extraversion vs. Introversion) gets the 3 and which gets the 4.

To help force the decision, you'll be provided with a chart outlining the strengths of each dimension. Following the chart will be a Thumbnail Personality Sketch Scorer for you to complete.

Thumbnail Personality Sketch

Attitude Toward Life	Extravert (E)	Introvert (I)
	Prefers to work with others Is reactive Speaks often and well Is action oriented Interacts well with others Is a broad-based thinker Enjoys the external	Works independently Is reflective Listens more, talks less Thinks before acting Concentrates well Is an in-depth thinker Enjoys the internal
Ways of Knowing	**Sensor (S)**	**iNtuitor (N)**

	Works well with details
	Is practical
	Is realistic
	Uses five senses to learn
	
	Is oriented to present
	Works patiently on routine
	  tasks
	Likes hands-on tasks
		Sees big picture
		Is creative
		Is theoretical
		Uses intuition and
		  imagination
		Is future oriented
		Likes new tasks to
		  solve
		Prefers conceptual
		  tasks

Ways of Deciding	**Thinker (T)**	**Feeler (F)**

	Doesn't let personal feelings
	  interfere
	Is objective
	Critically evaluates
	Sees logical outcomes
	Decides with the head
	Is firm but just
	Seeks correctness
		Considers the feelings
		  of others
		Is subjective
		Empathetically evaluates
		Sees effects on people
		Decides with the heart
		Is compassionate
		Seeks harmony

Orientation to the World	**Judger (J)**	**Perceiver (P)**

	Is decisive
	Plans life
	Controls the situation
	Likes closure
	
	Works at planned pace
	Decides quickly with
	  minimal facts
	Is task/mission oriented
		Is flexible and open
		Lives for the moment
		Adapts to change well
		Is curious and open-
		  ended
		Works in bursts of energy
		Decides based on depth
		  of data
		Is process oriented

SCORING EXAMPLES:

Let's consider two people: John and Mary.

John is outgoing and engaging. He loves being around people and gets a great deal of energy from them. He is articulate and always ready with a comment for just about everything. A very creative person, he sees the endless possibilities concerning all things in which he's involved. While he does not like the details of daily life, he can draw conceptual conclusions easily and is always ready to take on a new problem. Sensitive to the feelings of others, John is an empathetic friend and co-worker who decides with his heart more often than with his head. He seeks harmony within the workplace and provides inspiration and compassion wherever he goes. Finally, John decides issues easily and prefers to plan ahead so he can control whatever situation he finds himself in. He does not like surprises, seeks closure, and is very task oriented. In short, John is an ENFJ: an extraverted, iNtuitive, feeling, judger.

Here's what John's TPS Scorer might look like:

John's TSP Scorer

Attitude to Life	Ways of Knowing	Ways of Deciding	Orientation to the World
E=4 I=3	S=2 N=5	T=1 F=6	J=7 P=0

Mary, on the other hand, is a mirror opposite of John. She's very introverted and prefers to be alone in order to think—she gains energy and insight by being alone. She likes things that are concrete and physical, deals well with details, and has a strong interest in history and the here and now, not the future or what might be. She's a logical thinker and cares little about what other people think, only about what makes sense logically to her. She is organized, critical of herself and others, and firm but fair. Finally, she's more curious than closure oriented. She gathers large amounts of information when attempting to solve any problem. She's open-ended, often delaying a decision in favor of more input. In short, Mary is an ISTP: an introverted, sensing, thinking, perceiver.

Here's what Mary's TSP Scorer might look like:

Mary's TSP Scorer

Attitude to Life	Ways of Knowing	Ways of Deciding	Orientation to the World
E=2 I=5	S=6 N=1	T=4 F=3	J=2 P=5

YOUR TSP SCORER

Now it's time to score your own TSP. Remember the general instructions: You have 7 points to divide between each of the four pairs. Don't use fractions or decimals. You must make a choice, basing your decisions on your work persona. Refer back to the Thumbnail Personality Sketch on page 21.

Your TSP Scorer

Attitude to Life	Ways of Knowing	Ways of Deciding	Orientation to the World
E= I=	S= N=	T= F=	J= P=

You have just decided that you are one of 16 personality types identified by Myers and Briggs. From this you can easily determine which of the Four Basic Writing Types you are. Because writing is thinking on paper (a cognitive process), writing types are determined largely by their thinking or cognitive functions (S vs. N and F vs. T). Attitudes (E vs. I and J vs. P) will certainly affect a writer's style, but to a lesser extent. Therefore, your basic writing type will be the *middle two letters* of your personality type: SF, ST, NF, or NT. To illustrate, in the two examples, John's TSP Score indicated that he was an ENTJ; therefore, his basic writing type would be an NT. Mary's TSPS indicated that she was an ISTP; thus her basic writing type would be an ST. Determine your basic type by circling the two middle letters of your type from the TSP Scorer.

CHAPTER III

THE FOUR BASIC
WRITING TYPES

In order to get a concrete handle on these Four Basic Writing Types, I have given each the name of a particular writer which best personifies the types. For example, SFs are strong feelers who are sensitive to people; thus, I call SFs correspondents—those who frequently write more personal correspondence. STs, on the other hand, prefer scientific, logical writing; they are technical writers—those who like technically precise and scientific writing. NFs—the more creative, intuitive types—are the creative writers, those likely to write stories, novels, or more imaginative pieces. Finally, NTs, the intellectual thinkers, are the analytical writers, those who prefer writing that is more theoretical and logical. However, you must keep in mind that the degree to which people fit these descriptions will depend on the strength of the scores in the dimensions (0 to 7 points). For example, an ST who scored S as a 6 and T as 7 will more closely fit the description in the Thumbnail Personality Sketch than the ST who scored S as a 4 and T as a 4. In short, the Four Basic Writing Types are:

1. SFs — Correspondents
2. STs — Technical Writers
3. NFs — Creative Writers
4. NTs — Analytical writers

To illustrate these writing types we'll view four different people. First, you may recall the creative writer John (**ENFJ**) and the technical writer Mary (**ISTP**). Let's also introduce two other types: Donna, the correspondent (**ESFP**), and Jess, the analytical writer (**ENTJ**). The particular way each of them would attack the prewriting phase of writing will now be illustrated.

To help you understand these four types, I will discuss them individually in general terms, then discuss both their strengths and weaknesses, provide you with a few hints about how they are best used in organizations, and finally, offer a sample of writing likely to be produced by each type on the same topic: family leave for husbands.

Correspondents: Sensors/Feelers (SFs)

The first type of writers I'll discuss are the correspondents (SFs). Like all correspondents, Donna (E**SF**P) is a sensor (S), and concerned with collecting accurate, factual information. Moreover, she is comfortable with amassing data and documenting that data accurately. Because she is a feeler (F) and is concerned with pleasing people, Donna will focus on how others will feel when they read a passage. This concern with audience impact makes her a "pleaser." She chooses her words, examples, and arguments in order to create a favorable impression on the audience and to avoid anything that might offend the readers.

Correspondents' Strengths:

- *Factual writers.* Data is usually accurate and ample.

- *Audience centered.* High concern for the audience's feelings and wishes. Highly liked for their personal touch.

Correspondents' Weaknesses:

- *Lack conceptual approach.* Often have trouble drawing conclusions and grouping data in meaningful ways.

- *Will ignore logic.* If correspondents think that the logic of the situation is too harsh a reality for the audience to accept, these writers will forgo it in favor of a more palatable audience-pleasing argument.

- *Because of their overly personal touch, can be seen as mushy or softhearted.* Some may view them as weak and overly emotional.

Hints About Correspondents:

Have correspondents like Donna write personal and personnel pieces for your organization. Their writing will be warm and will be most concerned with how others feel. Letters of regret, customer satisfaction or complaint responses, and sympathy notes are among their specialties. Keep them away from writing adversarial letters or negative personnel actions—that's just not their forte, and they may not have the stomach to refuse or make a tough decision when needed.

Correspondent Indicator

A correspondent, Donna would compose a memo similar to the following:

To: All Supervisors
From: Donna

Subject: Helping Our New Fathers

Last year there were 17 cases in our organization in which men could have taken family leave to be with their newborn babies, but did not. In an attempt to provide our employees with the most humane policy, I suggest canvassing all employees for their suggestions. Your help in turning up accurate and dependable information on this company policy is appreciated. But the most important thing to remember is that we must work together to solve this problem because people must remain our central concern.

Technical Writers: Sensors/Thinkers (STs)

Mary (I**ST**P), a technical writer (ST), is a rule maker and rule keeper of writing. Concerned with facts and logic, she focuses on accuracy, accuracy, accuracy. Her concern with precision and logic, in fact, makes her a good editor and a stickler for good grammar.

As an editor, Mary "calls 'em as she sees 'em." If she sees something incorrect, she has no trouble telling you. Mary's writing conforms to traditional rules, and she likes traditional writing models and formats. Give her a writing format, and she will stick to it and will make sure that everyone else does until the rules officially change. For example, if you want company memos to start with the main point first, you can be assured that technical writers (STs) will do just that and will appreciate that you told them what you wanted.

Technical Writers' Strengths:

* *Excellent with facts.* Data are always correct and accurate. Enjoy working with facts and numbers. Are comfortable in the world of data. Can marshal information, remember it, and express it accurately and concisely.

* *Logical.* Arguments are rigorous and logical. Draw accurate conclusions based on solid evidence. Have few, if any, leaps in faith—their conclusions are grounded in fact.

Technical Writers' Weaknesses:

* *Could have difficulty with concepts.* Often obsessed with factual accuracy, technical writers (STs) have trouble developing themes and making conceptual groupings. Their writing is a mass of factual data which can leave the reader asking, "So, what does it all mean?"

- *Might be seen as insensitive.* Based on a high need for arguments and a strong sense of what is right or wrong, technical writers often polarize audiences with their writing because they take a "black or white" stand on issues. Their "here is how it is" tone of writing may offend readers who will view STs as cold, callous, and uncaring; therefore, readers sometimes reject the message out of hand.

Hints About Technical Writers:

Use writers such as Mary, who we would call a Sensor/Thinker, as stewards of rules and regulations. They're very good at reviewing writing and make excellent editors. They can make good decisions based solely on the facts they are given. Assign to them policy writing and the writing of rules and regulations, and they will thrive. Personal writing is not their strength. While they may see such writing as occasionally acceptable, they generally view it as mushy and unnecessary. When they write such communications, their writing comes across as artificial and insincere to readers.

When reviewing STs' writing, check for concepts. Have they pulled the facts together in a way that is easy for the reader to grasp the major points of the writing? Or, have they merely marshaled a litany of facts and figures? Make sure that their writing is audience based and does not read like a military General Order—unless that's the tone you want the writing to imply.

Technical Writer Indicator

A technical writer, Mary might write a memo similar to the following:

To: All Supervisors

From: Mary

Subject: Personnel Policy Changes

During Fiscal Year 92, 17 men who were eligible for family leave did not take it. Have all full-time employees fill out the following questionnaire immediately for suggestions about whether the policy should be changed and report that data to this office by August 1st.

Creative Writers: Intuitors/Feelers (NFs)

John (E**NF**J), a creative writer (NF), is a writer who seeks to write about what's new and different. He's concerned with what could be—possibilities—and with audience awareness and acceptance. He understands audiences superbly and is as adaptable as a chameleon, though he sometimes appears overly sensitive when placed in decision-making roles. However, as a writer, he can produce written copy as fast and interesting as any personality type. His writing is rooted in the conceptual, and his approach is novel, when and where possible.

Creative Writers' Strengths:

- *Creativity.* These writers like the challenge of a new project, a new piece of writing. They won't flinch at anything requiring a new approach; they also want to inspire and motivate others.

- *Audience-based.* Can figure out what an audience needs and provide it. Persuasive—they are great sales people. They strongly consider audience needs and try to fulfill them—the essential formula for sales and persuasive writing.

Creative Writers' Weaknesses:

- *Facts.* Always check the research, data, and facts collected by NFs. They mean well but aren't always exact and might even sacrifice a few truths to enhance the style and audience's acceptance of a piece. General concepts turn them on, not nitty-gritty facts and details. To NFs, such writing details are unnecessary evils. NFs seek to embellish and paint a picture as opposed to just listing facts as an ST may be inclined to do.

- *Logic of argument presented.* NFs' logic is based on arguments connected to values, not facts. Indeed, the concern for audience needs (a strength) can become a weakness when it overpowers the required logic of a writing piece. Creative writers (NFs) will sacrifice hard facts for the readers' feelings or to promote a value position—a tendency that may weaken a piece of writing.

Hints for Creative Writers:

Use creative writers (NFs) like John as your generators, creative initiators, inspirers, and cheerleaders. They make great writers as long as they get challenged with new problems and assignments. So vary their assignments, even if you have to give them writing outside their normal areas. Challenge their fertile imaginations, and you'll keep them producing and working for you for a long time.

Avoid asking them to perform repetitious assignments or to write rules and regulations, which will bore them silly. Remember that their writing is often emotionally a piece of them. Support them while they are writing, and tell them you appreciate their writing. Make sure they understand the value of the writing assignment to others.

Creative Writer Indicator

A creative writer, John would submit a memo like the following:

To: All supervisors

From: John

Subject: "Dads with Kids"

The birth of a new child is a special time in a family's life. However, many fathers in our organization are not taking advantage of our family leave policy. Since we believe that a strong nuclear family plays an integral part in our company and is the backbone of the American idealism, you are strongly urged to come to a meeting on Thursday prepared to discuss your ideas and feelings on this important subject.

Analytical Writers: Intuitors/Thinkers (NTs)

Jess (E**NT**J), an analytical writer (NT), is the most dominant, forceful of the writers. While she's creative (like John), her writing tends to be objective, even insensitive. Confident of what she logically knows, Jess expresses a self-assured tone in her writing. She has a great facility for idea-based logic and develops numerous possibilities in her writing. More often than not, Jess will end up as a leader in business, industry, or the military. NTs, like Jess, also often become scientists and college professors. In any case, they have no fear of expression and write often.

Analytical Writers' Strengths:

- *Intuitive.* See many possibilities in a piece of writing. Perceptive in an uncanny kind of way—able to make inferences from only shreds of hard data.

- *Analytical.* Have a strong sense of logic and clear-headed thinking. Good at problem solving. Use logic to address any data or information supplied. Good at reaching tough decisions in their writing because analysis and logic are their guiding lights. Architects of plans and policies. Good at pointing out abstract consequences and overall, big-picture planning.

Analytical Writers' Weaknesses:

- *Facts and data.* Make most of their errors while compiling data. Facts and data are of some value to NTs, but only in the context of supporting a particular thesis or position. They expect the reader to read between the lines. Don't be misled by forceful NT writing; check the data, facts, and documentation closely.

- *Coolness.* May appear to be insensitive to people when they write because they prize logic, not feelings or audience needs. Indeed, if NTs see something a particular way, they call it. This often appears in print as analytical, if not callous and insensitive.

Hints for Analytical Writers:

NTs, like Jess, appeal to audiences across the spectrum because they are both intuitive and analytical. They need help in becoming more sensitive to audiences. To take advantage of their writing style, give them writing assignments which require a problem-solving approach. On the other hand, be careful when they start slinging data around. Don't get too snowed by the force of their persuasive arguments. Ask to see the facts and documentation.

Analytical Writer Indicator

An analytical writer, Jess might write a memo like the following:

To: All supervisors
From: Jess

Subject: Leave Situation

Many fathers have not taken advantage of our family leave policy. I'm assuming this is because they've worked out a logical arrangement with their spouses to have their bases covered. I imagine many fathers are concerned that such leave negatively affects their careers and their competitive status in the organization, and therefore opt out. Let me know if my assumptions aren't correct.

In the next chapter you'll see how each of the Four Basic Writing Types uniquely approaches the writing process. From that perspective, you'll get a better look at how to coach and encourage them to be more effective writers. But, before that, here's a chart to help you pull this chapter together.

The Four Basic Writing Types

	Strengths	Weaknesses	Hints
Correspondents (SFs)	Factual Audience-centered	Lack conceptual approach Will ignore logic Appear mushy	Write personal pieces for organizations Keep away from negative writing that might offend Check writing for logic and ability to draw concepts and/or conclusions
Technical Writers (STs)	Excellent with facts and data Logical and rigorous	Have difficulty with concepts May be seen as insensitive	Good detail editors Use for policy writing Keep away from writing where warmth is necessary Check writing to ensure it is meaningfully conclusive and is audience oriented
Creative Writers (NFs)	Creative Possibilities oriented Audience-centered	Facts and data suspect, often inaccurate Logic often flawed in favor of audience acceptance	Vary writing assignments Give creative "new" assignments Keep away from overly historical or factual writing
Analytical Writers (NTs)	Intuitive Analytical	Facts and data. Appear cool and impersonal	Give assignments geared to theory Avoid personal writing tasks Check their data and often impersonal tone

CHAPTER IV

PERSONALITY TYPE AND THE WRITING PROCESS

Personality affects all you do—including your approach to writing. When it comes to the actual writing process, some techniques of thinking, writing, and editing work better for some writing types than others. You could be more comfortable with your writing by trying the techniques that suit your type. This chapter, therefore, will summarize the steps of prewriting, drafting and editing, and discuss how different personalities might best approach these different steps of the process.

Prewriting

The prewriting step includes all the early phases at the beginning of the writing task. During prewriting, writers define the topic and the audience and explore what they know about a topic. To discover such information, writers use various devices or techniques such as freewriting, freelisting, freespeaking, and freewebbing.

Freewriting

Anyone who has ever written a quick letter to a friend has practiced freewriting. It's a quick and nonthreatening method to get some initial thoughts on paper so that writers can find out what they already know before they begin to research their topics.

The rules are simple:

1. *Imagine that you're writing to a good friend—* someone who will not judge your writing harshly.

2. *Start writing to your friend and try not to stop until you've finished explaining your ideas in everyday language.* The objective of the exercise is to keep the pen moving and write what's on your mind.

3. *Don't stop to correct penmanship, spelling, grammar, or punctuation.* Remember that the purpose is to prime the idea-pump and keep the waters of the mind flowing.

EXAMPLE #1

Let's say you want to hire a new editor for your office and you must sell the idea to your boss. You decide to write a memo. If you find yourself at a loss for words, you might first try freewriting to a friend, Bill, who is less threatening:

Dear Bill,

We're in the market for a new editor to produce our weekly newsletter. This editor needs a solid grasp of grammar, proven editorial experience, and writing talent, as well as an ability to get along with people. We need this position filled now because our company has grown so quickly.....

As you can see, it's much easier to write a letter to a friend than to start right out talking directly to the boss. Words flow naturally and effortlessly.

Freelisting

If you've ever made a checklist, even a grocery list, then you've freelisted. This is another way for writers to get their ideas down on paper quickly without the clutter of excess words. Again, the rules are simple:

1. *Write your topic at the top of the page and begin to write down any ideas or words that you think relate to that topic.*

2. *Look over the original list and try to check off or highlight the main ideas.* You may find some insignificant ideas among the central ones. Don't toss them out completely—you'll consider them all again later.

3. *List each main idea on a separate piece of paper and repeat the process of listing any ideas you have about each one.* Now select the main ideas under each subtopic and repeat the process until you can no longer break sublists down any further.

4. *When finished, you'll have a long list of topics, subtopics, and even sub-subtopics as evidence of what you know before you take another step in the writing process.*

EXAMPLE #2

To illustrate freelisting, we'll again use the example of looking for a new editor.

New Editor

Why Need—

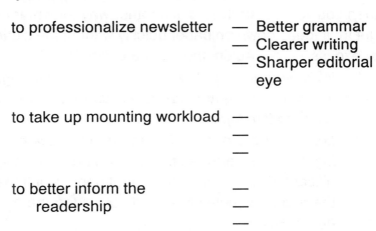

to professionalize newsletter	— Better grammar
	— Clearer writing
	— Sharper editorial eye
to take up mounting workload	—
	—
	—
to better inform the readership	—
	—

As you can see, freelisting begins to formulate an outline:

New Editor

I.   To professionalize the newsletter
   A. Better grammar
   B. Clearer writing
   C. Sharper editorial eye
II. To take up mounting workload
III. To better inform the readership

Freespeaking

Some people talk to *hear* themselves think. If you've ever talked to a friend about any topic in a casual and unstructured way, then you've used freespeaking. The rules are easy to follow:

1. *Go to a quiet room with a tape recorder.*
2. *If you can get a friend to listen to you, great.* However, if you can't or if you don't have the time, then just assume a good friend is sitting across the table from you.
3. *Begin to explain conversationally your topic and what you know about it to your friend.* Let the tape recorder run. Don't stop it, even if you hesitate.
4. *Review and transcribe the main thoughts and facts that came out as you spoke.* Now you have a place to start.

To see what transcribed freespeaking would look like, you need only read freewriting! The results of the two techniques are identical—only the process is different.

Freewebbing

If you've ever drawn a sketch or a diagram of a process on a piece of paper—even sketched an athletic play in the dirt—chances are pretty good that you've already done your first freewebbing. Here are the rules:

1. *Write the main topic in the middle of the page.*
2. *Free associate any thoughts related to the topic. Draw a box or bubble around each new idea. Connect the ideas with lines.*
3. *Continue to break down the subtopics by drawing off lines and bubbles in all sorts of directions leading to new thoughts.* Don't be afraid to list any spinoff ideas related to the topic. Just keep the

web going until you've spun it as densely as you can to catch all your new ideas and facts.

Let's look at what our example might look like if it were done using a web:

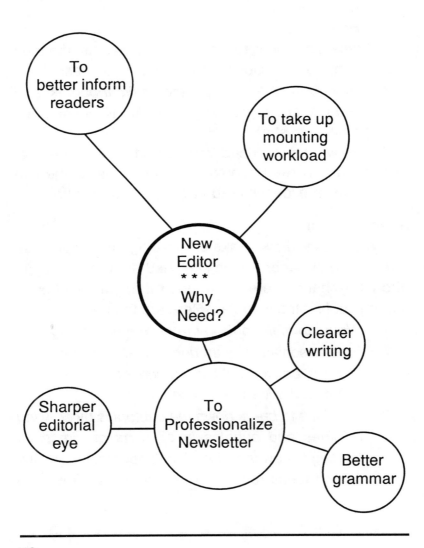

Personality and Prewriting

This section will discuss which of the different prewriting techniques might best suit each of the Four Basic Writing Types (correspondents, technical writers, creative writers, and analytical writers). In general, however, the best techniques for each will also depend on whether the type is an introvert or an extravert.

Introverts focus on the inner world of ideas. They energize from being alone; thus, independent self-contained activity appeals to them. When given writing tasks, introverts will usually first seek counsel from their own inner voices, not from others. Thus, the more internal prewriting techniques like freelisting, freewebbing, and even freewriting may appeal to an introvert. However, freespeaking may not appeal because it is an external technique, one often disliked by an introvert.

By contrast, the extravert may very much enjoy freespeaking because it involves other people, yet may not like more internal techniques like freelisting or freewebbing. Interestingly enough, many extraverts seem to like freewriting, perhaps because it's like letter writing to a friend and is people oriented.

With the idea of introversion and extraversion in mind, consider each of the Four Basic Writing Types as they begin the prewriting phase.

Correspondents (SFs)

You may recall from the previous chapter that correspondents can handle data and people (the audience) well. Therefore, it will come as no surprise that Donna (ESFP) would like to use freelisting (data centered) as a prewriting technique. ESFP's are also comfortable with people-centered techniques like freewriting and free-speaking.

Technical Writers (STs)

As a technical writer, Mary (ISTP) focuses on data and logic and prefers writing that is pure and simple, fact-based, and rational. Thus, she prefers data-centered, logical prewriting techniques. Specifically, Mary prefers freelisting above all other methods. Freespeaking does not appeal to her because that technique involves too much extraneous verbiage. Neither freewebbing nor freewriting appeal to Mary's neat-and-trim writing type because these methods appear sloppy, bloated, and unstructured.

Creative Writers (NFs)

Expressive, creative writers like John (ENFJ) com-municate naturally and love people; thus, they prefer forms of prewriting such as freespeaking, freewriting, and freewebbing. However, freelisting seems a bit cold and impersonal; so it is not John's technique of choice. Quite the opposite of Mary—John, a creative writer, does not mind any technique requiring innovation because he is open to experimentation and an audience-centered approach and does what it takes to appeal to that audience.

Analytical Writers (NTs)

As an analytical writer, Jess (**ENTJ**) is conceptual and logical. She may like all four techniques. On one hand, she likes the clear logic of freelisting. On the other, she also likes the conceptual freewheeling of freewriting, freewebbing, and freespeaking, especially because she is extraverted.

Prewriting Personality Styles

	Prefer	Dislike
Correspondents **SFs**	Freewriting, Freelisting, Freespeaking	Freewebbing
Technical Writers **STs**	Freelisting	Freewriting, Freespeaking, Freewebbing
Creative Writers **NFs**	Freewriting, Freespeaking, Freewebbing	Freelisting
Analytical Writers **NTs**	Freewriting, Freelisting, Freespeaking, Freewebbing	

Drafting

Writing the actual drafts of a particular piece of writing is called drafting. This step consists primarily of two phases: research and revision. Research consists of activities that develop the topic beyond what authors bring to the table, based on their personal experiences and knowledge. Research may involve as little as talking to a few experts who know the topic well, or it may consist of sophisticated testing, measurement, and extensive literature and database searches for the most current information available about the specific topic.

Revision, the second phase of drafting, deals with those changes made to prepare original writing for the audience. Beginning with prewriting, writers revise according to their writing types. The most important aspect of revision is structure, both on micro- and macro-organizational levels. On the micro level, structure means organized sentences and paragraphs. Having clearly connected sentences and paragraphs organized by topic sentences makes the piece cleaner, clearer, and easier to read. Structural organization on a macro level focuses on coherency with respect to the overall piece—connecting not only paragraphs but also whole sections. Quite simply, structure demands an answer to the question, "Is the writing organized so that the reader can comprehend it quickly and easily?" With the concept of drafting in mind, let's see how each of the Four Basic Writing Types would face this step in the writing process.

To illustrate how the Four Basic Writing Types might approach drafting, I'll use an example of how the four types would individually handle the assignment of writing a memo on the upcoming company picnic.

Correspondents (SFs)

As a correspondent, Donna (**ESFP**) likes to focus her research on facts and data, and she's very interested in her readers' needs. Always fearing that she might offend her readers, she spends a lot of time determining the correct tone and voice for a piece of writing. Because she's an extravert, much of Donna's research may come from interviewing and asking others about the topic. When she writes a draft, she will prefer to appeal to audience needs rather than taking a straight, logical, and concise track.

Correspondent Indicator

A correspondent, Donna might compose a memo like the following:

To: All Supervisors
From: Donna

Subject: Family Fun Picnic

On August 26, the company picnic will be held at Bushy State Park. The fun will include water games, volleyball, and enough grilled ribs for the entire family. The cost is only $10 a head for adults, $3 for children. So bring the whole family and spend the day basking in the sun!

Technical Writers (STs)

Mary (**IST**P) prefers working with facts and numbers, and she likes to do so logically, taking a more direct, if not impersonal, approach. In general, Mary will quote well-known, classic documents and rely on established examples. Her research and resulting data will be impeccable; she prides herself on accuracy and the authority of her sources. Her collection and structural methods will be logical, regardless of audience appeal. Her primary concerns are accuracy of facts and logic of the argument. As an introvert, she prefers to think extensively about her topic, thinking things through and then writing one or perhaps two drafts. But don't look for her to enjoy extensive revision. As far as structure and organization are concerned, her writing will always follow a readable, classic, predictable, if not boring, style. Don't look for any structural innovations from Mary, but you will get writing that is clear and logical—depend on it.

Technical Writer Indicator

A technical writer, Mary might submit a memo like the following:

To: All Supervisors
From: Mary

Subject: Company Picnic Information

The company picnic will take place on Saturday, August 26, from 11 a.m. to 7 p.m. or dark, whichever comes first. The cost is $10 a head for adults, $3 for children. Games include volleyball and various water sports. The menu is grilled ribs.

Creative Writers (NFs)

A creative writer, John (**ENFJ**) naturally enjoys writing and communicating but not researching details. His idea of research is brainstorming about a subject. He merely tolerates facts and details, unlike Donna (**ESFP**) and Mary (**ISTP**). John's facts and documentation are often questionable, a claim to which he may often shrug his shoulders and say, "You get the general idea, don't you?" Moreover, he can tolerate a sloppy first draft or two. Then, as an iNtuitor (**N**), he is inclined to move on to something new. John is not a perfectionist by nature, but his writing evolves into maturity during the drafting step, much more so than the other basic types (SF, ST, NT). Also, because he focuses largely on his audience,

55

he'll often sacrifice logic to promote his values and persuade his readers.

Creative Writer Indicator

A creative writer, John might submit a memo like the following:

To: All Supervisors
From: John

Subject: Annual Family Picnic

On August 26, the company will hold its annual family picnic from noon till whenever. The costs are minimal. The menu will include quality family time, as well as great food like grilled ribs, various salads, and some sort of dessert. We need your ideas for activities, please submit a few and get involved!

Analytical Writers (NTs)

As an analytical writer, Jess (**ENTJ**) is a conceptual writer. She will seek and value understanding and try to accurately depict a particular concept, but her facts may be flawed because data are not her forte. She's uncomfortable with minute detail and tends to group information into logical categories to make sense of it. She can draw conclusions and meaning from facts and data better than any of the four types. Concerning structure, Jess's sharp sense of logic wants writing that is clean and logical, however conceptual it might be. Such writers also possess excellent vocabularies and like to use them.

Analytical Writer Indicator

An analytical writer, Jess might submit a memo like the following:

To: All Supervisors
From: Jess

Subject: Annual Picnic

On Saturday, August 26, Bushy State Park will host our company's annual picnic. The cost is $10 for adults, $3 for children. A repast of grilled ribs is planned with games to follow. Directions are available in the front office; think about coming.

Drafting Personality Styles

Types	Research Method	Structure Style	Overall Preferences
Correspondents SFs	Focus on facts, data May conduct interviews	Correct tone, voice are important so as not to offend others	Appeal to audience needs, rather than logistical concerns
Technical Writers STs	Rely on classic examples and well-known documents Accuracy, logic are important	Follow a predictable, if not boring style. No innovations	No extensive revision. Clear and logical
Creative Writers NFs	Conceptual Facts, documentation often questionable	Use drafts to work through a piece	Will often sacrifice logic to promote and persuade
Analytical Writers NTs	Facts may be flawed. Lack detail; group items instead	Dislike revision, yet concerned with concise, logical product	Draw conclusions well. Possess excellent vocabularies

Editing

The final step of the writing process is the editing step—making those final touches to a piece of writing that bring it to closure. This step is the most mechanical one in the writing process—one in which writers often work alone, but should not. In an upcoming chapter I'll discuss, in depth, a new method of group revision and editing.

Closure is an important concept for both personality and writing. In fact, the fourth personality typing dimension (judgment vs. perception) in personality typing relates specifically to closure.

Myers and Briggs referred to this dimension as the attitude taken toward the outer world. Judgers (Js) are people with a strong sense of closure who prefer to develop a plan and then live by it. They have a strong need to be in control. Once they have set a time schedule, they want to stick to it and do not like anyone to interfere.

On the other hand, perceivers (Ps) have a strong thread of curiosity and wonder running through them. They prefer things open ended and flexible so that they can adapt to the changing nature of life. Instead of driving toward closure, perceivers keep their options open. Accordingly, they dislike planning because they feel restricted by the process; rather, they like to take life one day at a time.

It should be no wonder that such personality dimensions have a strong effect on the editing phase of the writing process—where writing comes to an end. Often judgers (Js) will end the process a bit too soon in order to meet a deadline and keep to the scheduled plan. As a result, they may omit significant research and discussion—in a sense, stop before the product is fully developed. On the other hand, judgers will work at a planned, paced rate, accomplish many tasks, rarely be late, and meet stringent deadlines.

However, strong perceivers (Ps) may keep a project going long after any useful outcome is likely. Ps will work in "fits and spurts" to meet a deadline (if they meet it at all) rather than "steady as she goes" like Js. Their sense of curiosity leads them to research and discover new facts and concepts useful to complete a thorough piece of writing. In short, perceiving and judging, like the other three dimensions (extraversion vs. introversion, sensing vs. intuition, and thinking vs. feeling), bring both strengths and weaknesses to the writing process and need to be considered, especially when editing.

To show how the Four Basic Writing Types might edit a co-worker's material, I'll demonstrate how each type might edit a paragraph on recycling.

Correspondents (SFs)

Naturally detailed people, correspondents keep a sharp eye on facts and figures in any piece of writing that they edit. As editors, SFs also demand that the writing reflect a warm, personal tone appropriate to the relationship with the reader. Donna (ESFP) might likely ask herself: "How would the reader react to this piece of writing?" As a sensor (S) she might also ask: "Are these facts and figures for this piece of writing absolutely accurate, and are they taken from reliable sources?" Her personality ensures that she will focus on these important questions as she edits. However, preferences, and the strengths that accompany them, result in weaknesses as well. For example, because Donna has a strong sense of feeling (F), she may allow some errors to slip through the cracks during the editing process in order not to offend the writer. Moreover, Donna is a perceiver (P) and has difficulty completing a piece of editing or writing. She has trouble with deadlines and often wants an extension in order to get more details to complete any task. But, it's often questionable whether or not what she's going after is worth the wait.

Correspondent Indicator

A correspondent, like Donna, might edit in the following manner:

Correct spelling please

Recycling in the Uited States has become more and more popular in the past decade. Bins of aluminum and glass sit at the end of every driveway. Huge recyclers at gas stations are fed daily with thousands of items. Gas attendants pump the gas while people recycle. By incorporating the entire family into the program, a valuable lesson can be taught while saving the environment at the same time.

Great – Include the family!

Technical Writers (STs)

The technical writer is a natural-born editor. For example, Mary (ISTP) has a keen eye not only for detail, like Donna (SF), but also has a strong sense of structure and logic. When editing a piece of writing, she considers facts, details, and accuracy to be as important as logic, flow, and conciseness of the argument. As effectively as STs edit, they can evoke emotional responses from those who may react to their matter-of-fact, abrupt, and often insensitive editing. STs must learn to develop "people" skills so that the importance of their message is not lost in the coolness of their editing style. Unlike Donna, Mary is a judger (J) and does not need to be monitored because she is driven to complete the task at hand. However, it's also well worth remembering that Js, in their zealous drive for completion, may often overlook the need for additional new data or a particular approach which might later prove vital to a piece of writing.

Technical Writer Indicator

A technical writer, Mary, might edit in the following manner:

Spelling error —

Recycling in the Uited States has become more and more popular in the past decade. Bins of aluminum and glass sit at the end of every driveway. Huge recyclers at gas stations are fed daily with thousands of items. Gas attendants pump the gas while people recycle. By incorporating the entire family into the program, a valuable lesson can be taught while saving the environment at the same time.

Can you document this? Illustrations?

Is this accurate?

Do you have any exact figures?

this is not needed.

This ¶ takes up valuable space, but says little.

Creative Writers (NFs)

While they are naturally creative writers, NFs are neither natural nor comfortable editors. Take John (**ENFJ**), for example. His pen is always ready to write—particularly in broad, conceptual, intuitive (**N**) strokes; however, he'd rather have a root canal than to edit either his own or another's piece of writing. First, he does not work especially well with detail; he prefers the broader, more conceptual approach to life in general and writing in particular. Second, when editing someone else's writing, as a feeler (F), John may often overlook errors for fear of hurting the writer's feelings. Further, while he has a strongly developed sense of feelings and values, John has an underdeveloped sense of logic and analysis. This does not mean that he is either illogical or unanalytical. However, because he spends so much time using and developing his feelings and values, he tends to underuse or underdevelop his logical, analytical side.

John is also a judger (J), which brings, as with the perceiver (P), both good and bad news. The good news is that John will always bring a piece of editing together by the deadline—without fail. He is decisive, an organizer who plans his work and then works his plan. However, on the down side, he may be so wedded to his plan that, even if a new and important side issue arises or if the work takes a turn in another direction, John is more willing to give up curiosity for closure, sometimes leaving a gaping hole that should be filled.

Creative Writer Indicator

A creative writer, John, might edit in the following manner:

Spelling ☺

Recycling in the Uited States has become more and more popular in the past decade.Bins of aluminum and glass sit at the end of every driveway. Huge recyclers at gas stations are fed daily with thousands of items. Gas attendants pump the gas while people recycle. By incorporating the entire family into the program, a valuable lesson can be taught while saving the environment at the same time. ← *Nice Job!*

Is this the right spacing?

Good image!

Good image!

← *Good image!*

Good to focus on family- and shared values

Analytical writers (NTs)

Generally take-charge kinds of people, analytical writers will also take charge when it comes to editing. People who tend to think they're always right, NTs like Jess (**ENTJ**), have a clear sense of logic, direction, and purpose in their editing. They know what they want; they go for it; and, they can be very critical of others. As mentioned, NTs are also very conceptual and will have a strong sense of overall order and organization. They can easily come up with central, controlling themes and have no problems with organizing a piece of writing. However, they are neither the best at detail nor good at documentation editing—their minds are simply not geared to dotting *i*'s and crossing *t*'s. Moreover, with their strong sense of logic, NTs often have an under-developed sensitivity to readers. Translated, this means that when NTs edit, they need to be more careful not to offend writers or misjudge their needs. NTs have a problem having their work edited by someone they don't consider as competent. As a card-carrying judger (J), Jess has all the same qualities as John who is also a J, and whom we just discussed. In short, Jess is good at planning and deadlines, but she needs to keep her plan a bit more flexible and open ended to account for unan-ticipated data and directions that may be important to her editing.

Analytical Writer Indicator

An analytical writer, Jess, might edit in the following manner:

SP.

Recycling in the U~~nit~~ed States has become ~~more and~~ more popular in the past decade.Bins of aluminum and glass sit at the end of every driveway. Huge recyclers at gas stations are fed daily with thousands of items. Gas attendants pump the gas while people recycle. By incorporating the entire family into the program, a valuable lesson can be taught while saving the environment at the same time.

Not Necessary

— What about paper?

— All passive voice. Sounds weak!

To help pull all Four Basic Writing Types together for you, the chart on the next page summarizes their editing strengths and weaknesses:

Editing Personality Styles

	Strengths	Weaknesses

Correspondents SFs	Sharp eye for accuracy
	Demand the piece have
	  a personal tone
		May have problems seeing
		  big picture
		May allow errors to remain
		  rather than offend the
		  author

Technical Writers STs	Keen eye for detail Sound structure, logic	May not have a good over- all concept Often insensitive editors

Creative Writers NFs	Broad-based conceptual
	  editors
	Well developed sense of
	  audience, values, and
	  feelings
		Not good with detail editing
		Underdeveloped sense of
		  logic, analysis

Analytical Writers NTs	Good conceptual editors
	Demand a clear sense of
	  logic, purpose, and
	  organization
		Not best at detail or docu-
		  mentation editing
		Can be overly critical

SPECIAL NOTE

The Four Basic Writing Types are convenient ways of looking at writers. Certainly, people may vary from these descriptions based on many factors, such as culture and education, not to mention the intensity of their scores in each dimension. Nonetheless, having a way to look at writing systematically can create tremendous potential in the work setting.

But, beyond the Four Basic Types, you should also consider how personality attitudes (Extraversion vs. Introversion and Judgment vs. Perception) will affect those four types. For example, an extraverted correspondent, who is also a judger, will approach a writing assignment much differently than will an introverted, perceiving correspondent. Thus, these attitudes can add insight into how people write, based on their personality types.

CHAPTER V
WRITERS' PERSONALITIES WITHIN THE ORGANIZATION

Organizations are dynamic and diverse—change is a key word today. It's not a one-flavor world, and diversity should be celebrated, not mourned. Therefore, we all must learn how to recognize, embrace, and use diversity of personality to make change work for us. We each have different personalities. The central theme of this book is that diversity of personality affects writing in significant ways. Because you spend many of your conscious, and perhaps unconscious, hours at work, and because many of those hours are spent writing, it makes sense to explore personality typing at work.

This chapter will first discuss the Four Basic Writing Types at work, the professions where they are most often found, and where inside a typical organization you may discover them. You'll also get some type-spotting techniques—ways of identifying different personality types within organizations. Of course in the absence of having people accurately tested by using a validated instrument, no system will be totally reliable; however, you will be able to make educated guesses, based on what you'll learn in this chapter, that will give you some insight when dealing with different personalities within your organization.

Moreover, by being able to identify types at work, you're more likely to understand various writing types—their strengths and weaknesses. At the same time, by understanding type differences, managers can begin to think about organizing and assigning teams for writing projects to cash in on the strengths offered by diverse personalities. How writing teams work in collaborative groups will be discussed fully in the next chapter.

Personality Types at Work

Every day you run into different personality types at work. Instinctively you may know they're different, so you adjust to them. You've met the softhearted secretary who wouldn't hurt a soul. She's the kind of person who cares about everybody's problems. Then there is the company auditor who is precise and accurate about everything she does. You may view her as a "bean counter" who has little time or concern for anything emotional. She seems aloof, even cold. Varieties of personality energize our society and our organizations. In fact, certain personality types in a particular job, may work well. In addition, different personality types all can fit together and work to complement each other in effective, quality organizations which celebrate differences.

How organizations fit personalities together on problem-solving teams or within working units is essential to maximize both personal and organizational potential. You may recall previous discussions in this book of how the weaknesses of certain personality types were the strengths of others. Therefore, if you can learn to spot different types, you'll be better able to buttress your type with the help of another whose strengths may complement your personality.

To illustrate the Four Basic Writing Types in the workplace, I will give examples of the assets they bring, common career paths they choose, and how to pick them out from among your co-workers and employees.

Correspondents (SFs) at Work

The warmest of personality types, correspondents (NTs) are practical, down-to-earth realists who like other people. They are the team builders and nurturers in the workplace. Strong on feeling (F), they need and seek a harmonious workplace and will strive to compromise and accommodate in order to maintain that harmony. Correspondents generally want to serve. They work well when they believe that people like them but tend to take criticism personally. They are also practical people who are comfortable with facts and numbers but uncomfortable with abstract concepts or creative ventures.

Correspondents offer organizations several important keys for success: stability, group maintenance, and work effort. First, let's look at correspondents who are loyal and dependable. They hold onto jobs for long periods of time. As company and personal loyalists who stick around for the long haul, correspondents are not easily wooed away by fame, fortune, or fanciful promises.

Second, they enrich group maintenance—so important for the survival and productivity of any organization. Getting the job done (task orientation) in an organization is important, but keeping the players together in harmony or unity (group maintenance) is equally important for an organization to remain healthy and productive. Indeed, correspondents, with their caring for harmony and their strong sense of feeling for people, maintain the group in very concrete ways. They will often send cards to or call people when they are sick, are concerned about how someone is feeling both emotionally and physically, and are frequent contributors of their time, talents, and money to the social aspects of the workplace. For example, they are often the first to volunteer to host a birthday or promotion party and are equally willing to help out if illness or tragedy strikes.

Third, they are the workhorses of the organization. They work well with detail and tedium because of their love of data and information. Unfortunately, they tend to take on jobs and problems of those around them and can be targets for abuse and overassignment. Not ones to complain, correspondents will work in silent desperation, overwhelmed by all that people have dumped on them. They are steady players in the workforce, always ready to help on a work-related or personal problem. In short, correspondents are the best friends an organization or person can have.

Because of their attention to detail, their down-to-earth nature, and their strong affinity for harmony and people, correspondents are most commonly found in service industry organizations in general. For example, many correspondents populate social work organizations, elementary schools, hospitals, community service institutions, and the like. Within organizations in general, they will occupy such service-oriented positions as nurses, child-care workers, secretaries, and health-service positions. They also gravitate to hobbies and leisure-time activities which often involve helping people, like volunteer work, coaching, and tutoring.

Personality types like correspondents do not generally gravitate to executive positions largely because such directive, leadership positions often require difficult choices—decisions which could hurt people's feelings and which might disrupt the harmony that correspondents so enjoy. Corresondents are invaluable to any organization.

To spot correspondents in your organization look at particular positions within your organization, look at a person's workspace, and listen to how they communicate. First, you need only look at people in support positions. For example, you're more likely to find a counselor, nurse, or receptionist as a correspondent than a doctor, lawyer, or engineer. Second, the office of a correspondent is usually warm, personal, and comfortable. You'll often find pictures of family and friends on the wall or on a credenza. Often they also keep collectibles which have sentimental meaning. When they communicate (speak or write) they use many personal pronouns—"I" and "you." Their conversation almost always begins with a question about how you and your family are feeling or doing.

Correspondent Indicator

ASSETS BROUGHT TO WORKPLACE:
- loyalty, dependability
- group unity promoters
- workhorses of the organization

COMMON CAREERS:
- service industry positions
- nurses, secretaries, child care workers, social workers

HOW TO SPOT IN THE WORKPLACE:
- maintain a warm office setting
- enter into personal communication with co-workers

Technical Writers (STs) at Work

The coolest of personality types, technical writers are the ultimate realists whose need for detail and logic overrides their need for harmony. Technical writers are the auditors of life. They prefer accountability, analysis, and research as ways of expressing their interests. They find absolute comfort with numbers and data, and they treat the information with the cold eye of logic. If something does not make sense to them, they devalue it. Their cool eye for factual logic often elevates them to leadership positions—many technical writers become CEO's or presidents of organizations. They also gravitate to work that focuses on their strength of data and analysis, such as accounting, law enforcement, research, science, and engineering.

Technical writers bring to the organization several important factors: analysis, accuracy, and compliance. First, they bring analysis. Because of their affinity for data and its logical application and interpretation, technical writers bring an analytical and problem-solving approach to any issue. Their first question is likely to be, "What are the facts?" They don't get sidelined by emotional red herrings, and they keep their wits about them in the most heated of emotional situations. Seen as cool headed and collected, they are excellent spokespersons in tense situations; however, they are not the best ones to express emotion or caring.

Second, technical writers bring accuracy to organizations. Their love of data makes them good stewards of information. They like data to be accurate and will spend time and effort to make sure that it is. When someone finds a flaw in their data, technical writers get upset with themselves. However, don't look for them to admit error easily, because they spend so much time working at being correct.

Third, compliance is important to technical writers. They like rules and people who follow them. They prefer to establish rules and guidelines and make sure that they are followed by their subordinates. Their organizations tend to be administratively tight. Also, they are quite comfortable with punishing anyone who violates the rules.

Personality types like technical writers naturally seek executive positions because they enjoy tough-minded decision making that is based on information and logic. With little need for personal popularity, or for harmony, technical writers easily make the toughest of decisions with little personal anguish. In short, technical writers are the best rule makers, auditors, and administrators that an organization can find.

To spot technical writers in the organization, look at people in referee-type positions such as auditors, inspectors, military officers and administrators who show a strong fondness for detail. Technical writers' offices are usually meticulous and Spartan. Little adorns their walls, and interior objects are often compulsively ordered. Their motto could be: a place for everything and everything in its place. They also tend to be quite conservative in their office attire. Not given to the fanciful, they tend to dress in traditional clothing that is meticulously clean.

Technical Writer Indicator

ASSETS BROUGHT TO WORKPLACE:
- analysis
- accuracy
- compliance

COMMON CAREERS:
- executive/administrative positions
- auditors, lawyers, analysts

HOW TO SPOT IN THE WORKPLACE:
- are referee-type workers
- maintain Spartan offices
- dress in traditional attire
- have a no-nonsense attitude

Creative Writers (NFs) at Work

Among the warmest and most creative personality types, creative writers are freethinking, innovative, and people-oriented players on the organizational team. Creative writers "push the envelope" of change in any organization. Just as the correspondents and technical writers seek tradition and stability, creative writers seek change and variability. Looking at what *could* be and not what is, their eyes are usually fixed on the future of the organization, rather than on its past. They are not rooted necessarily in the nuts and bolts, facts and data of daily life—rather in concepts and ideas. Possibilities-oriented, creative writers scoff at consistency being the "hobgoblin of little minds," as Emerson reminded us. Focused on people's reactions (feelings), creative writers seek a harmonious and nurturing environment.

Because of their special orientation toward intuition and feeling, creative writers also bring special traits to organizations: enthusiasm, creativity, and cooperation. If they don't like a particular situation, they recreate it. Life for creative writers is a series of new possibilities. For creative writers, reality does not merely exist. Rather, it is recreated—by them.

Along with enthusiasm and creativity, creative writers bring a cooperative spirit with them. Heavily invested in feelings, they are sensitive to their audiences—both personal and corporate ones. They read audiences well and will work toward resolution of conflict through cooperation rather than confrontation.

Based on their idea-centered and people-oriented nature, creative writers can often be found occupying influential positions within an organization. Their nature is to influence, inspire, and change thought. Thus, they are most often psychologists, trainers, public relations specialists, and consultants. They also abound as writers within any organization.

To spot creative writers in an organization, look for persuasive people and also those in the positions just mentioned: psychology, training, public relations, and consulting. To identify creative writers, listen for those people who often talk about the importance of the future and change. They use terms like "what if" and "why not" and "let's give it a try." Their offices are steeped in variety and possibility. You'll find walls filled with a variety of hangings—a potpourri of ideas and concepts. For example, you might find an abstract painting alongside a performance award. You may find a picture of them shaking hands with the CEO and a pair of lottery tickets that "just missed" stapled to the wall. They seek uniqueness, often dressing flamboyantly or at least in a way that gives them a special "signature." It may be a handkerchief in the pocket or a scarf off the shoulder, but there is usually a signature aspect about creative writers' dress in particular and their lives in general.

Creative Writer Indicator

ASSETS BROUGHT TO WORKPLACE:
- enthusiasm
- creativity
- cooperation with others

COMMON CAREERS:
- influential jobs
- trainers, consultants, public relations

HOW TO SPOT IN THE WORKPLACE:
- are future thinkers
- are persuasive
- have unique offices and dress styles

Analytical Writers (NTs) at Work

The most intellectually rigorous of types, analytical writers ask the ultimate "what if" questions. Often thought of as visionaries, they are usually concerned more with an organization's future than its past, and more about possibilities than scientific reality. They base their curiosity in the world of research—theoretical research. As such, analytical writers are interested in sweeping change and broad theoretical concepts as opposed to accuracy on a practical level. Because they rely on logic as a filter for incoming information and outgoing decisions, analytical writers may appear to be cold and aloof, much like the technical writers.

Like other personality types, analytical writers also bring to any organization unique and valuable gifts: potential, analysis, and leadership. First, the notion of potential needs to be discussed. Due to their broad-brush, theoretical nature, analytical writers see potential and possibility in all situations. Because of their philosophy to try life's options, many tend to become theoretical scientists and inventors. Second, analytical writers, like technical writers, also rely heavily on analysis; however, both types start at two very different places. Technical writers begin with data and work to a conclusion—inductive reasoning. The analytical writers begin with conclusions (overall meaning) and work down to the details—deductive reasoning. While technical writers draw conclusions from data, analytical writers draw new knowledge and concepts from old concepts and knowledge. Third, analytical writers provide leadership in the world. Many of them serve in leadership positions in America's institutions. Because of their tremendous vision of the future, their strong intellectual capacity, and their persuasive argumentation skills (logic), they gravitate to the tops of organizations.

Therefore, you'll likely find analytical writers as leaders of businesses or organizations. They also show up as trial lawyers (as opposed to research attorneys), scientists (theoretical), and college professors. Within organizations, you'll find them as leaders in executive positions. They will show up as managers of dynamic organizations. If organizations are not dynamic before they take over, they are when analytical writers leave.

Analytical writers can be found in a variety of departments within an organization such as legal counsel, research, and wherever theory and logic intersect on the job. To help spot analytical writers, listen to them talk. Most analytical writers will refer to a "broad-brush" approach and use words like "possibilities" and "logic." They will talk frequently about ideas and concepts, but less about facts and details. Their offices are often filled with books on a wide range of topics. They dress functionally and are rarely flamboyant. Most analytical writers could not care less about appearance—it's too mundane.

Analytical Writers

ASSETS BROUGHT TO WORKPLACE:
- innovation
- analysis
- leadership

COMMON CAREER:
- organizational leaders
- lawyers, scientists, professors, executives

HOW TO SPOT IN THE WORKPLACE:
- talk of ideas, not facts
- dress functionally
- appear abrupt, cold, aloof

Conclusion

Obviously, different basic personality types think, act, and write differently based on their internal programming; however, if you know or can intelligently recognize personality types, you'll be at a distinct advantage in any relationships or dealings that you have with others. This chapter should have served as an attempt to give you a snapshot of the Four Basic Writing Types in an organization. Because it's very unlikely that most of the people that you meet will have their personality types tattooed on their foreheads, it's important that you are able to recognize the Four Types when you encounter them within your organization. There are two reasons. First, if you work for someone, you'll need to know that individual's personality type in order to deliver your product, written or otherwise, in a manner acceptable to him or her. Second, if you supervise people with varying personality types, you'll need to know their strengths and weaknesses as people and as writers as soon as possible.

Personality and the Workplace

	Assets Brought to Workplace	Common Careers	How to Spot in the Workplace
Correspondents SFs	Are loyal, depend-able. Promote group unity. Are the workhorses of the organiza-tion	Work in service positions Examples: Nurses, secretaries, child care	Look for service workers, warm office setting, per-sonal communica-tion with coworker.
Technical Writers STs	Good with problem solving, analysis, accur-acy. Like rules and those who follow them	Work in executive/ administrative positions Examples: Auditors, attorneys	Look for referee-type workers, Spartan offices, traditional attire
Creative Writers NFs	Are enthusiastic, creative. Work well with others, cooperative	Work in influential jobs. Examples: Trainers, consul-tants, psychologists	Look for persuasive people, future thinkers. Offices and attire are daring, creative
Analytical Writers NTs	Will try anything rational. Provide analysis, logic, and leadership.	Work as leaders Examples: Trial lawyers, scientists, professors, execu-tives	Look for leaders who talk of ideas instead of facts, dress functionally and approach life theoretically

In the next chapter you'll learn how to harness the energy and value of diversity when you begin to apply it to a piece of writing.

CHAPTER VI
COLLABORATIVE WRITING GROUPS

Having learned how to spot different personality types and where you might find them in your organization, now you must learn how to use them collaboratively to produce the writing you want. Actually, the philosophy behind this collaborative writing is quite simple, but effective: Diversity in small writing groups generates an improved writing product. Most of us know the old adage that two heads are better than one. In fact, research shows us that three to seven heads are quite a lot better than one or two heads and that a group of five people is the ideal. Having fewer than three people in a small group tends to reduce the group's effectiveness, because they don't generate the interplay and power of five people with diverse personalities. On the other hand, a group of more than seven is too large to either coordinate or control. The bottom line: small, diverse groups work. In fact, the more dissimilar the personality types in a writing group, the more likely they will be a good test audience for your writing. When discussing writing groups, two questions usually arise: (1) How do you put together an effective writing group? and (2) How do they function in order to be productive, not destructive? This chapter will answer both of these key questions.

Selecting a Writing Group

To select an effective writing group, go back to the basics that you've learned about personality. Remember that diversity means power, and start with the Four Basic

Writing Types as the best mix for an initial cut for your group. If possible, try to have a correspondent (SF), a technical writer (ST), a creative writer (NF), and an analytical writer (NT) in your writing group because the richness of their distinct personalities will provide you with a test audience that represents virtually the entire span of thinking styles. It's helpful to know that a piece of writing has been reviewed and accepted by the "world" (at least in terms of personality types) before you spring it on your intended audience.

To staff your group, I suggest that you find a group of peers who work together in the same office, and who know your topic, to help reduce the time necessary to learn the topic. Further, such a collaboration of working cohorts makes for a more cohesive atmosphere in the office, as well as one that is more reciprocal—"you help me with mine, and I'll help you with yours."

Diversity provides a powerful review. The ideal situation to ensure personality diversity is to have all group members take either the Myers/Briggs Type Indicator or Thumbnail Personality Sketch. Once you start practicing your own profiling, it becomes progressively easier. Even if you're not completely accurate, you still have the benefit of many different eyes looking at a piece of writing. You may not have the time or the diversity to get each of the basic types into your writing group. Do the best you can, which will be infinitely better than what most people do to ensure diversity—nothing. Also, when selecting personality types for your group, attempt to balance extraverts and introverts in your group. Too many extraverts can result in people fighting for talk time; too many introverts can result in no talk at all.

Question: Should groups be ad hoc or permanent?

Answer: It depends.

If you are in an office that often writes involved and complex pieces, I strongly suggest establishing a permanent group because it facilitates the writing process. Group members will learn the ground rules and know that there is a tomorrow and that their papers are next. This tends to keep people committed to doing a good job and not slacking off. Certainly, there are permanent writing groups—people who meet on a regular, if even social, basis to share pieces of writing, either professional or personal. Such groups are usually willing to review a piece of writing; however, they often do not have the subject-matter expertise necessary to give a particular piece of writing a complete review. For an expert review you may want to get an ad hoc group together at work to review the document.

Making Writing Groups Productive

Having selected a writing group, it's now important to understand how to make the group productive, not destructive. Indeed, a poorly run group can do as much to destroy writing as to enhance writing. To get the process rolling, take the following preliminary steps:

1. *First and foremost, have the writer produce as clean a draft as possible.* Nothing upsets

reviewers more than to have to correct basic errors created by a sloppy writer who chooses to use a group to *rewrite,* not just review, a piece of writing.

2. *Give people time to review the draft.* Distribute a clean draft to group members well in advance of the conference day chosen so that they may use it to discuss the writing.

3. *Schedule the meeting at a convenient time.* Remember that group members have other things going on in their lives besides reviewing some-one's writing. All group participants should bring a marked-up copy to the meeting.

4. *Choose someone other than the writer to lead the group.* The writer has too much at stake to be objective or to run the meeting effectively. Any other group member may suffice; however, you may wish to pick someone who you know will keep the meeting on track. If possible select a leader with a personality type that matches your principal audience. For example, if the writing is for your boss who is an NT, you may wish to choose a person to lead your group meeting who is also an NT. Of course, this luxury may not always be available.

5. *Find a convenient place to conduct the meeting.* This location should be away from distractions like phones or any interruptions which could distract the group. Often, an office or conference room

away from the general flow of business will meet the need. If the meeting must be conducted in the office itself, ensure that no calls come in or go out except in an emergency.

The Four Basic Types in Writing Groups

Next, you must be aware of how the Four Basic Writing Types will respond, in a group, to the writing of another—and how they will react to criticism of their own writing.

Writers have different ways of responding and reacting to criticism. To illustrate this point, quotes follow each type discussion, giving examples of how various types might respond to another's writing or react to criticism of their writing.

Correspondents (SFs) in Groups

As *responders* to others' writing, correspondents will always try to find the bright spot. Concerned with the feelings of others, they will attempt not to hurt writers' feelings and will also try protect the audience's feelings. Hesitant to confront, correspondents will talk around issues by asking questions like, "How would it work if you tried...." They will also likely comment on the accuracy of research and the particulars of writing, such as spelling and grammar.

As *reactors* to criticism of their own writing, correspondents can be easily hurt. They need to know whether or not you liked their writing first, and then if you like them. Acceptance is important to them and vital to their writing.

The accuracy of their data is a source of pride. To respond effectively to correspondents, make sure you keep in mind their keen interests—data and feelings.

Correspondent Indicator

A correspondent might say:

As Responder:
"I can see you researched this topic very thoroughly."
"Your opinions were helpful. Perhaps you could include a few more."

As Reactor:
"I'm so glad you enjoyed the piece!"
"Yes, I did conduct extensive research on my topic. I'm glad it shows!"

Technical Writers (STs) in Groups

As *responders* to others' writing, technical writers are the most critical, blunt, and detailed. Their orientation to detail and facts (sensing) and their interest in logic and analysis (thinking) frame how they both give and accept criticism. When responding they are likely to comment on: accuracy, detail, reliability, documentation, logic, and analysis. Their approach is direct and blunt. Not pre-disposed to be sensitive, technical writers' directness can unintentionally injure more sensitive writers.

As *reactors* to criticism of their own writing, they can accept direct criticism if it is supported by facts, details, and logic. Opinion that is not strongly supported is rejected as meaningless. To respond to technical writers, consider their strengths and concentrate on them before moving into new areas of criticism. For example, you might want to tell them what details are working well, even what details you might challenge based on your direct experience, before asking them to consider providing a conceptual overview at the beginning of the document. They will be better able to accept a discussion about "overview" and "concepts" after you've dealt with them in their comfort zones—data and logic.

Technical Writer Indicator

A technical writer might say:

As Responder:
"Where did you find this quote? I don't understand it."
"You need to proof your work. Your errors detract from the product."

As Reactor:
"That may be your opinion, but the facts say something different."
"I researched my thesis at the Library of Congress."

Creative Writers (NFs) in Groups

As *responders* to others' writing, creative writers are much like correspondents in that they seek harmony and are sensitive to the group's and the audience's feelings (F). Also, not given to direct confrontation, creative writers will try not to attack writers and are more likely to ask questions. They'll tell you their *emotional* reaction to the writing and try to affirm the writer (unless their values are offended). Interested in the conceptual (iNtuition), creative writers are predisposed to the innovative and the creative and will likely make comments on those aspects during the meeting.

As *reactors* to criticism of their own writing, creative writers also tend to be rather sensitive and often take criticism personally. They have trouble separating the writing from themselves. Therefore, groups should use caution when commenting to them—by first establishing good will (talking about what worked well) before providing criticism. While this technique is important for all writers, it is doubly true of the strong feelers—creative writers and correspondents. Be careful of offending creative writers' values and let them know that you *appreciate* their efforts or point of view. To respond to creative writers, take time to commend them on their innovation, creativity, sensitivity, and the heartfelt tone of their writing before you launch into the criticism of their data and logic, which often warrant revising.

Creative Writer Indicator

A creative writer might say:

As Responder:

"I have never seen this approach before, but
I like it!"

"Your writing style is very unique!"

As Reactor:

"I'm pleased you can see my viewpoint on this
subject."

"No, I used a completely different approach this
time."

Analytical Writers (NTs) in Groups

As *responders* to others' writing, analytical writers bear a resemblance to technical writers in that they tend to be direct, often bluntly so. In short, analytical writers are critical reviewers. Because they possess a strong sense of logic (thinking), they see little use in dancing around issues; rather, they prefer to get to the heart of the matter. Analytical writers will focus on innovation and the conceptual arrangement of the writing and are often obsessed with structure. They will be the hard chargers of the group and may need to be reined in by a particularly strong group leader lest they run roughshod over writers.

As *reactors* to criticism of their own writing, analytical writers can be particularly stubborn. Their forceful, "take charge" personalities can often blind them to their own weaknesses and intimidate others as well. To respond to analytical writers, you should use care to approach them and ask direct questions, both about their data and the audience—these two areas seem to be soft in the work of an analytical writer. Reviewers need to prove their own competence first to be credible to an analytical writer. They like to hear that their writing shows a creative, innovative approach and that it makes sense. Lead with such comments if they are appropriate.

Analytical Writer Indicator

An analytical writer might say:

As Responder:
"The structure of this article needs to be reworked."
"Did you think before you wrote this? Your thoughts skip from page to page!"

As Reactor:
"You liked the new format? I'm pleased you noticed."
"What do you know about this subject?"

Conducting a Group Meeting

If all preliminary steps went well, you have your writing group seated around a conference table prepared to discuss the writing. Before the group discussion begins, there are two things group leaders must do:

1. *Turn on a tape recorder.* By recording the discussion, you allow the writer to capture those invaluable offhand remarks that people make during the course of discussion. Moreover, the recording will capture the interplay and emotional reaction of members which may emphasize certain critical points but which are often forgotten in revision unless there is a recording to remind the writer.

2. *Ask the writer to discuss what went well when writing the piece.* This allows the anxious writer to talk about and give excuses about writing—all of which helps the writer calm down. Keep in mind that writers generally feel vulnerable and, therefore, apprehensive during the review process. Further, writers will often focus in on what is wrong with their writing. Leaders should stop any such negative self-flagellation and remind the writer to talk first about what worked well in the writing.

Before that discussion begins, you should know two things about writers in general. First, a critique of writing can be like discussing what's wrong with you—a most personal and potentially intrusive conversation.

Second, writers must be prepared psychologically for criticism; you must reduce anxiety and show trustworthiness to gain their confidence. To do this, group leaders can employ a three-step, C-A-H approach: *Commend* the writer, *Ask* questions, and *Help* the writer with specific suggestions. Remember, to critique another's writing you must first "earn the right" to offer that criticism. Just as you would not walk up to a stranger and tell her what an ugly suit or dress he or she was wearing, you must also avoid jumping headlong into a diatribe about another's writing. Each of the critique procedures explained below moves from the least intrusive to the most intrusive step as the critic gradually earns the right to offer criticism. To ensure a productive, not destructive meeting, here are steps for the review process:

1. *Commend the writer.* To do this the leader should provide a good example. Thus, the leader might begin by saying: "I was impressed by the way you introduced and explained the nature of the problem...." Note that the leader starts to commend by pointing out a specific facet of the writing, rather than by offering a commendation such as, "I really thought your writing was interesting, *but*...." Such perfunctory openings are viewed as insincere, patronizing, and merely a ploy to launch into a full fledged diatribe. After leaders have opened the discussion positively they should invite group participants to comment: "Let's go around and discuss what each of you thought worked well in the writing." By methodically asking each participant, leaders ensure comments from even the most introverted people—an important technique that will help to get the most out of what the group has to offer. Often, introverts have well conceived

thoughts and opinions, but will not express them unless asked to.

Other troubles may arise during the discussion. Extraverts, for example, may try to dominate the conversation, not because they are rude, but because they just like to verbalize every thought. Leaders must politely interrupt and move on to the next person by saying something like, "Thanks, Joe. Let's move to Mark so everyone will get a chance to comment during this first round. We'll all have other opportunities."

Another problem arises when certain impatient members want to get right to the weak spots in the writing. So, rather than leading with commendation, they will want to move right to "helping." Politely but firmly, leaders need to stop this behavior immediately lest the group process be killed before it is ever fully born. To halt this behavior, leaders might just say, "Thanks, Mary; however, what we're talking about is what worked *well* in the piece. What did you see that worked well?" These types of comments show the group that leaders are serious about the format for comment.

2. *Ask questions.* Again, leaders should model the behavior by asking questions that arise from the writing. For example, leaders might pose questions like, "What did you mean when you wrote....?" or "Can you explain the subtitle on page four?" The beauty of this asking technique is that

many writers will "self correct" when asked to clarify their writing. Self correcting is a willing response to change without having been told to. In the group setting it may sound like this: (writer responding to a question) "Oh, I didn't realize that people would not understand what 'ontogeny' means—maybe I should use a different word or at least define that one up front to avoid confusion." Having writers correct themselves (self correct) is much easier and less traumatic than telling them to do so.

3. *Offer help to the writer.* To do this, approach it again in the form of a question to the writer: "What gave you the most trouble while writing this piece?" Such an open-ended question will likely surface many of the problems that reviewers would have raised; and when the writer raises them, the group only has to agree with the writer if appropriate. It is much easier for writers to accept what they already believe to be true. If the writer does not bring up other necessary areas on which to comment, group members can offer suggestions like: "What if you moved the first paragraph...." or "Did you think about just leaving out section three completely?" Of course, by this time in the discussion group, members will have earned the right to offer help (suggestions for improvement) and to tell the writer what presents problems.

Final Revisions

Following the meeting, the writer should take the marked-up copy from each group member, along with the audiotape, and use them to revise the writing. Now, instead of resenting the changes to be made, the writer is more likely to accept them.

When deciding which changes to make, writers should employ the "Duck Theory" of Revision: If it looks like a duck, waddles like a duck, and quacks like a duck, it's probably a duck! Often writers have difficulty knowing exactly what advice to follow when they listen to the tape and read the marked-up copies. Problems arise when they have some people telling them to do one thing, and others saying something different.

Using the "Duck Theory" of Revision helps resolve conflict. First, if remarks about a particular point all converge then people liked it, understood it and you should keep it—don't mess with it. It works. Second, if there is general consensus that most did not understand or disliked a particular portion of the writing, dump it or revise it. It does not work. If the group is divided fairly evenly, then the writer decides. This happens infrequently; but when it does, it's best to let the author control the decision. Using the "Duck Theory" resolves conflicts quickly and objectively—resulting in a piece of writing that will float on any pond!

Personalities in Writing Groups

Types	As Responders	As Reactors
Correspondents SFs	Try to find the bright spot Concerned for others' feelings Comment on details like spelling, grammar	Can be easily hurt. Have keen interest in comments about data and feelings
Technical Writers STs	Are critical, blunt. Focus on logic, detail, accuracy	Accept well-supported critiques. Accept criticism better if complimented first
Creative Writers NFs	Seek harmony between group and author. Look for creativity and avoid attacking the writer	Are sensitive to critique. Like to be commended on creativity before data is picked apart
Analytical Writers NTs	Critical reviewers. Do not like to skirt the issue. May run roughshod over authors	Are stubborn, often blind to their own weaknesses Reviewers must prove competent before criticism is accepted

CHAPTER VII

THE CARE AND FEEDING OF PERSONALITY TYPES

Different personality types contribute significantly to any organization, and they should be nurtured and used to good purpose. As the old adage goes, "Different horses for different courses," and knowing which horses to put in which races and which to team together is especially critical when an important writing project needs to be completed.

For the most part, people in organizations write in isolation. In fact, a very basic value taught early in our school systems is that independence or "doing your own work" is revered. Thus, many people fear the loss of integrity if someone else corrects their writing—that somehow outside input to writing has violated some time-honored code of ethics. While nothing could be further from the truth, such strongly held myths work against a collaborative atmosphere. Instead, a competitive atmosphere results, which ultimately can become divisive and unproductive. Witness the current battle between the United States and Japan centered on two very different production philosophies: the United States' competitive philosophy versus Japan's seemingly more collaborative approach.

To be productive in any organization, you need to be concerned with the organization as a whole. Depending on where you are on the table of organization—assuming you're not at the entry level or the CEO—you have people below you, at your level, and above you. Thus, building collaborative relationships up, down, and across your organization can produce much stronger written products. This chapter will discuss the issue of how to nurture writers in your organization. Specifically, I'll look at this issue from the perspective of a supervisor.

Quality in the workplace is much discussed these days. Getting people at every organizational level to realize the significant roles they play in serving customers is the goal of today's dynamic companies. Consumers will buy products from companies that "do it right." And, while there is no right or wrong way to write, there are ways to ensure that people collaborate to produce a quality product that will keep readers coming back.

In a very real sense, supervisors must learn to become coaches—not because it sounds right, but because the idea of being a coach fits the philosophy of collaborative writing so well. Think about it: coaches work with players "where they are" and always strive to coach them to a level of play where coaches would like those players to be. However, good coaches know what they can change, what they can't change, and have the wisdom to know the difference between the two. Workers come to supervisors like players on a team turn to their coach, ideally all working toward the same goal—making the organization a success. Supervisors must motivate all the players on their teams to play to capacity; and if they are exceptional coaches, they will get players to perform over their heads—reaching for stars and finding them. Therefore, the obvious question arises: How do supervisors get the best out of their teams? The answer: Supervisors must be good coaches. Yes, but how?

First, establish a sense of ownership. Assign projects to be written and then allow people the room to work. Neither hound them, nor let them float adrift. Discuss projects up front. Agreeing early on about the project's direction will keep it on course and avoid clashes later. Give people independence to write in a way that is best for them. In some cases, particularly where judgers (Js) and perceivers (Ps) are involved, this may cause stress. For example, Ps often leave the final writing until the last moment because they need the stress of an upcoming deadline to finish a project. On the other hand, Js tend to finish projects well before the deadline because their comfort comes from completing a task.

Finally, regarding responsibility, avoid the temptation to appropriate text. Often people develop the philosophy, "It's easier just to do it myself...." In writing, this philosophy gets acted out when supervisors literally steal a project back from the person assigned the task. This usually happens because the supervisor perceives that the person assigned the writing task is in over his/her head—either overworked or not capable of handling the assignment. Such text appropriation often ends in disaster—the supervisor gets overworked, and the writer becomes resentful and eventually unproductive.

Instead of appropriating text, supervisors need to support people by encouraging peer-support writing groups. As discussed in the previous chapter, the basis for selecting peer group members is personality difference or diversity. The idea behind such peer-centered review is that these differences will add to a piece of writing, not detract from it.

When building a peer group, seek out people fitting each of the Four Basic Writing Types. Such a universal mixture represents virtually any general audience's personality. Testing their products in such a peer-support group gives people a safe place to experiment with their writing creativity before going public.

This peer-review process will work in any organization dedicated to producing quality documents. Such groups not only provide a safe test audience, but also organizational expertise, internal political advice (what approach may work with which target audience), and subject-matter expertise.

However, this is not always easy to implement. The competitive nature of people often seeps into peer relationships. You may find yourself competing for resources and personnel; thus, you may be unwilling to point out your flaws and weaknesses to peers for fear that such exposure could be used against you to someone else's political advantage. While product competition in the marketplace may be beneficial, internal collaboration should be the name of the game before it gets to the market. The rule is simple: collaborate internally; compete externally. In terms of writing, this means that leaders must collaborate with their peers before proffering a piece of writing.

Coaching the Four Basic Writing Types

Good leaders are good coaches, and any good coach knows that all players perform at different levels. People also come at different writing levels, from novices to experienced writers, and supervisors must recognize clearly those differences when coaching them. For the sake of discussion, let's say there are two different writers: Sam and Karen. Sam is a new employee, fresh out of college—bright, but inexperienced. We'll call him a new writer. On the other hand, Karen is a career employee who's been with the company 15 years, knows the organization well, and has written numerous complex documents. We'll call her very experienced. When a supervisor gives assignments to these people, each with differing levels of writing experience, supervision must also vary to accommodate their experience levels.

For example, let's say that a new proposal has to be written that is complex, important, and requires knowing the company well. Obviously, Karen should get the assignment. And, when she's given the proposal to write, a supervisor should give it to her, ask what she needs, and step aside. Karen should not get help unless she specifically asks for it. Experienced and motivated writers want to be left alone to do their work. They simply want the resources that they ask for—research assistance, computers, travel funds, and the like—and then they need to work without interference.

On the other hand, if a relatively routine piece of writing is called for and requires little organizational savvy, Sam's the likely candidate for the job. But Sam will want and need supervision. First, he'll need (and want) specific step-by-step instructions. Because he may be unsure of the format and substance of the piece, his supervisor needs to stay close to him when giving any assignments, especially written ones. Providing people like Sam with the context and specifics of a piece of writing is essential. He must be told exactly what is needed, who the audience is, and the exact purpose for the writing. After he begins the writing process, a supervisor should check on him regularly and ask for interim products like outlines and rough drafts. This will make him more confident that he's on the right track, rather than waiting until the last moment to find out whether he hit or missed the mark.

The bottom line: experienced writers should require much less direct supervision than newer ones. Obviously, if older employees are not motivated to do a good job, then the problem is not writing, but management. The supervisor then must deal with motivation and discipline.

But, supervisors legitimately might ask, "How do I specifically coach the Four Basic Writing Types?" The answer is, in a word, differently. As I mentioned, different types require different approaches. Let's look at the Four Types briefly. We'll look at how to talk to them and what types of writing to assign them. But before we do, let's look at a matrix that reviews the strengths and weaknesses of each type to have that information firmly implanted before discussing how to work with them.

The Four Basic Writing Types—An Overview

	Writing Strengths	Writing Weaknesses
Correspondents SFs	Prefer facts, research, audience centered, caring, and warm	Lack concepts and creativity; appear too emotional
Technical Writers STs	Prefer facts, research, and logic; rules, formats, and discipline	Lack concepts and creativity; appear insensitive and cold
Creative Writers NFs	Are intuitive, creative, articulate; audience-centered, caring, and warm	Are weak with facts, research, logic, rules, and formats
Analytical Writers NTs	Are intuitive, conceptual, creative; analytical, and logical	Are weak with facts, research, audience-centered, rules, and formats; ignore values, feelings

Based on these strengths and weaknesses, supervisors must know how to coach each type and what kinds of assignments to give them. To do this, I'll provide another chart; but first, here are some general guidelines:

1. *Each type requires something different.*
2. *People do not remain static, especially with respect to experience.*
3. *Give respect:* show people you care about them personally and about their writing.

4. *No advice is foolproof.* Experiment and go with what works.

What follows is a chart which will give any supervisor coaching tips for the Four Basic Writing Types. It also provides assignment requirements most likely to be favored by each type. This by no means should indicate that people can or should only write certain types of assignments. Rather, it provides guidance for writing style preferences and for nurturing them among various types of writers.

How to Coach Writing Types

	Coaching Tips	What to Say...	Preferred Assignments
Correspondents SFs	Be careful of their feelings. Commend them, let them know you like them— this is key to their type. Look closely at logic and concepts	"I appreciated the attention you gave to the personnel memo, it was very helpful. Yet, I feel it would be more easily understood by readers if...."	Writing which requires: feeling, a factual basis, research, audience analysis
Technical Writers STs	Be direct and accurate. Say what you mean, play by the rules, and always be fair and equitable across the board. Watch out for lack of concept development and audience appeal.	"Your last article was written and documented well, but a few of the concepts need to be developed further. Could we discuss these issues?"	Writing which requires: rules, logic, research, a traditional format and/or scientific approach
Creative Writers NFs	Commend their creativity. They want to have their work accepted, respected and appreciated by their audiences. Look out for suspect data, inaccuracies, and faulty logic	"The new focus column you created is a real hit. It certainly livened up the old format. Could you show me the sources you used?"	Writing which requires: creativity, ideas, audience analysis, an innovative approach, and a conceptual approach
Analytical Writers NTs	Focus on innovation as well as the conceptual and structural framework that they develop. Watch closely for cold, impersonal tone and faulty data	"The memo you left on my desk was well written and in perfect order Could you use a more personal tone due to the sensitivity of the topic?"	Writing which requires: innovation, ideas, analysis, structure, a conceptual approach, and logic

CHAPTER VIII

Q & A ABOUT WRITETYPE

This chapter attempts to clarify and advance knowledge about WriteType in order to help you become a better, more informed writer who will know how personality affects the writing process.

What follows are some frequently asked questions about personality typing and about writing and personality:

1. **Q. What are the estimates of type distributions among the population?**

   A: Extraverts   75%
   iNtroverts   25%
   Sensors   75%
   Intuitors   25%
   Thinkers   60% Males, 40% Females
   Feelers   40% Males, 60% Females
   Judgers   55%
   Perceivers   45%

2. **Q: What are the estimates in the general population of WriteTypes based on cognitive styles?**

   A: SFs (Correspondents)   29%
   STs (Technical writers)   25%
   NFs (Creative writers)   28%
   NTs (Analytical writers)   18%

3. **Q: How can you determine your personality type?**

   A: First, you might consider taking the Myers-Briggs Type Indicator from a certified administrator. Centers which certify trainers include the following: Kroeger Associates, 3605-C Chain Bridge Road, Fairfax, VA 22030, (703) 591-MBTI; The Center for Applications of Psychological Type, 2720 N.W. 6th Street, Gainesville, FL 32609, (800) 777-2278; Consulting Psychologists Press, Inc., P.O. Box 10096, Palo Alto, CA 94303, (800) 624-1765; Type Resources, Inc., Suite 135, 101 Chestnut St., Gaithersburg, MD 20877, (800) 456-6284; and Growth Associates, 1901 East 1st St., Newton, KS 67114, (316) 283-2400.

4. **Q: Does personality type change?**

   A: No and yes. No, because, according to Jung, basic personality is inborn—preferences are ingrained at birth. However, as we work at different jobs, particular skills and preferences are developed while others are left undeveloped. But, an adaptation does not a new personality make!

5. **Q: Isn't typing writers or personality reductive?**

   A: Theory cannot explain all of reality, and it would be a gross error to try to explain all human differences in terms of personality or writing type. People are simply too complex for that kind of pigeonholing. However, personality typing does provide useful and reliable information for dealing with people. While you should never rely solely on personality typing or WriteType, you should not ignore what these tools may provide you: insight into understanding people. Just remember that people are more complex than the Four Basic Writing Types of WriteType or the 16 types of the Myers-Briggs Type Indicator.

6. **Q: Do certain writing types clash?**

   A: Yes. Interestingly enough, however, the types who tend to clash actually desperately need each other, but often can't figure their needs out until it's too late. With respect to the Four Basic Writing Types, the following pairs would tend to clash: STs and NFs have trouble seeing each other's points of view, and NTs and SFs also have similar troubles. Why? Simply because they process and experience life much differently. By the way, what I've said does not in any way mean that these types can't get along, only that these are the types most likely to have stormy relationships. Further, it also does not mean that similar types won't disagree either.

7.   **Q: What do you do when a writing group does not work?**

   A: When groups don't work, the answer is to change them or at least ask why they don't work. If there is a logistical problem or a lack of commitment on the part of one of the participants, then that problem has to be administratively approached by the leader. However, if there is a basic personality conflict within a group, then you should look at the personality types in the group and determine what type might better substitute for a person (or people) who seems to drain the group's power. I urge you to reread the chapter on groups before you decide to form a writing group.

8.   **Q: What books or materials are available for future reading about personality?**

   A: The following items are available:

   1.   *The Type Reporter*—this is a newsletter published eight times a year which deals exclusively with personality types (524 North Paxton St., Alexandria, VA 22304, (703) 823-3730).

2. The Center for Applications of Psychological Type, (800) 777-2278; and Consulting Psychological Press, Inc., (800)
624-1764, publish and sell numerous
types of materials, including books and
booklets, that will expand your knowledge
of personality. Among them are: *People
Types and Tiger Stripes: A Practical
Guide to Learning Styles,* by Gordon
Lawrence (1982); *Gifts Differing,* by Isabel
Briggs Myers and Peter Briggs Myers
(1980); *TypeTalk,* by Otto Kroeger and
Janet M. Thuesen (1988); and, *Please
Understand Me,* by David W. Keirsey and
Marilyn Bates (1984). Also available on
the topic of the teaching of writing and
personality types is *Personality and the
Teaching of Composition,* by George H.
Jensen and John K. DiTiberio (Able Pub-
lishing, Norwood, NJ).

9. **Q: Will knowing my WriteType solve my writing problems?**
   A: I wish it were that easy. However, writing is a
   skill that develops when you write. Knowing
   your type and the types of others will give you
   tremendous power when you do decide to
   write. And yet, neither knowing your type, nor
   sleeping with this or any other book under

your pillow, will ever make up for plain old practice.

10. **Q: Where do I go from here?**

   A: First, start writing. Second, try to join or form your own writing group. If you start your own, remember to use the "Thumbnail Personality Sketch" and blend types in the group. Make sure not only to have a mixture of the Four Basic WritingTypes, but also to have a balance of introverts and extraverts. Meet regularly and don't be afraid to discuss problems when groups are not working. Most of all, enjoy your newfound WriteTyping power.

Epilogue

Some final words need to be said about personality typing. First, you should know that such typing is not meant to pigeonhole people. That is, being a technical writer (ST) does not mean that a person is necessarily uncreative, anymore than being a creative writer (NF) means one cannot pay attention to detail. As I have mentioned, we all have each dimension to some degree or other, admittedly with stronger preferences in some dimensions than others. Moreover, whether you use WriteType's Four Basic Writing Types or the 16 Myers-Briggs types for convenience to discuss personality, each type has variances within it. While two individuals of the same personality type might look alike, they will also display differences based on a number of factors, such as culture, gender, age, and other variables.

Second, while WriteTyping is a useful tool for each of us, both as writers and supervisors, we must ethically make use of such information. Often, there is the temptation to want to know how people think in order to control them. This is not at all the purpose of personality typing—especially WriteTyping. On the contrary, WriteTyping seeks quite the opposite: to allow people to understand themselves and others.

Finally, writing is a skill that we all can develop. I firmly believe that no one is born a writer, only made one by effort and education. WriteType is my attempt to help people understand how they write, so that they can improve their own writing as well as the writing of others.

By being aware of differences, writers can be liberated from self-doubt and anxiety. The result is freer writing that encourages people to write more, which works to help improve their writing. Improved writing then makes people want to write more, and this self-reinforcing cycle repeats itself until a writer truly is born or reborn.

REFERENCES

Gladis, S. D. *Processwriting: A Systematic Writing Strategy.* Amherst, MA: Human Resource Development Press, Inc., 1989.

Jensen, George H. & DiTiberio, J.A. *Personality and the Teaching of Composition.* Norwood, NJ: Able Publishing Company, 1989.

Jung, C. G. *Psychological Types.* [translation, 1823]. Princeton, NJ: Princeton University Press, 1921.

Keirsey, D. with Bates, M. *Please Understand Me: Character and Temperament Types.* Del Mar, CA: Prometheus Nemesis Book, 1978.

Kroeger, O. & Thuesen, J.M. *Type Talk.* New York, NY: Delacorte Press, 1988.

Lawrence, G. *People Types and Tiger Stripes: A Practical Guide to Learning Styles.* Gainesville, FL: Center for Applications of Psychological Type, Inc., 1982.

MacDaid, G. P.; McCaulley, M. H.; & Kainz, R. I. *Myers-Briggs Type Indicator Atlas,* Gainesville, FL: Center for Applications of Psychological Type, Inc., 1986.

Myers, I. B. & McCaulley, M. H. *Manual: A Guide to the Development and Use of the Myers-Briggs Indicator.* Palo Alto, CA: Consulting Psychologists Press, Inc., 1985.

Myers, I. B. with Myers, P. B. *Gifts Differing.* Palo Alto, CA: Consulting Psychologists Press, Inc., 1980.